MORE PRAI

MW01199047

I wish I could wea. [poems] in this gorgeous debut like armor because I swear they are made out of silk and guts and mischief and happiness and hope and jokes and heartbreak and patch and rasp and ruin and wink and stray and stay and "millions of suns" and thin strange roads and holes and strong wings. They are as down to earth as they are untouchable. With these poems on, I think we might get out of here alive.

Sabrina Orah Mark

I don't know where to begin praising *Life After Rugby*, so I'll begin outside it, and say it reads like a culmination of much American poetry of the last twenty years ("every America / making its mark"), though this never seems to weigh it down, though it so often seems light, effortless even, though it is always perfectly itself. At the end of the book, G'Sell writes, "I have made light of many things / and that's why we can see in here," and when I read those lines for the first time, suddenly I did see: this is a fully realized, and therefore rare, debut, and a lifetime of a book.

Shane McCrae

Here, the play of language and what might be "made light of" leads to authentic truth and beauty under other names and in other forms. We find it in pop culture, the colloquial, the reality of lives lived, and the surreal and transcendent inside the quotidian. These poems make us look and listen, then elicit double takes, as any given line might be one "that lifts her word for skirt from the page."

Dora Malech

LIFE

AFTER

poems by

RUGBY

EILEEN G'SELL

GOLD WAKE

CONTENTS

I.

Follow the Girl in the Red Boots   3
Women & Children   4
The Reason the Moon Moves   5
Blanket Praise   6
After Camus Comes Out of a Coma   7
Last Night Alive   8
Ilona's Eyelids   9
Real Butter   10
Caution   11
Deep Space Dialectic   12
Ode to Clint Eastwood   13

2.

Like Good News from a Pretty Girl   17
The Hit   18
Sunday   19
Take Her Down   20
Explicit   21
Catastrophe Was Quite Polite   22
All Epics Are Disappointing
and All Disappointments Tend to Be Epic   23
Whitney Houston Pronounced Dead at 48   24
Nobody's Winter   25
Life After Rugby   26

3.

Euphoria Takes One for the Team   39
I Like That You Don't Care About Money   40
Through My Teeth   41
Not For Profit   42
"Little Boy"   43
Blessed Are They, the Cinematic   45
Faith Equivalent to Airplane   46
Love Poem from Detroit   47
Living Proof   48
Ode to Mike Tyson   49
Never Landing   50
Whoopi Will Always Be Center Square   51
Honeymoon That Never Happened   52
Impervious to Avalanche   53
Gently Now, the Revolutions   54

4.

Drive   57
Simple Plans   58
The Lonely Art of Collecting Olives   60
The Spring of Things   61
Ode to Taxi Driver   62
Melody, Speed, and a Man Worth Manning   63
Canoe   64
Ode to Roman Holiday   65
Invisible Men   66
The World   67
Closure   68

World Cup 69

Ode to California Chrome 70

From the First Book of Far Away 72

I Am, As Always 73

I Have Not Been Charged for the Closet 74

to Beti, Nishaa, Lissie, and Puffin

The love of beauty of the world . . . involves . . .the love of all the truly precious things that bad fortune can destroy.

~ Simone Weil

There's nothing more deadly and proficient than a happy fighter.

~ Mike Tyson

1

FOLLOW THE GIRL IN THE RED BOOTS

This place is weird, sexless, and white.
This is the place I came from.
This is the place from which I came.
Plenty of people have.

I am tired of "Du bist wunderbar."
I am smart as snow on Valentine's night.
I am a place of silt and lonely anecdotes.
Plenty of people are.

Forget what the head waiter told you.
Forget every plate you forgot to lick.
Forget dessert and disconsolate girlfriends.
Plenty of people do.

I have tried to redress December.
I have softly unbuttoned my Cacharel.
I have circled the dawns with erasable ink.
Plenty of people will.

Follow the girl in the stolen shoes.
Follow the map that she made you.
Follow the soar of her certain song.
Plenty of people won't.

WOMEN & CHILDREN

This world is filled with women and children. They are lifting, spitting. They are blocking the sun. They are dirtier than you ever remembered—holier, too. Done up, gone out. When one of them heads to the front of the line, the equator twists into taffy. Low-level clouds play tricks on rain; mountains sweet talk snow.

There were boats we used to put them in. They had years to drift so far, so good. They had ways with words, with wind, with flame. We warmed our mouths with impossible love. But when time arrived to take them back, no one knew what to talk about. Like the sound of a soda can opened

in space, their song released and detained our ears. What more could the good world offer us? What else would we ever truly deserve? Maybe the reason the moon moves on is only because we notice it. On quiet horses, the women and children are storming the city today.

THE REASON THE MOON MOVES

I've sat beside her. I've learned her name.
When Genevieve was only six, her father
died one evening. An electric storm cloud
swallowed her lunchbox. Neighbor children
buried her shoes.

I was born in 1979. I had very few
delicate baby outfits. My attentions
were coolly divided between a hunger
for truth and a taste for toppings.

A lack of quality opera lyrics
brought me to a standstill. Trains fled
the town of thought; my legs ached
a static madness. I saw a girl skipping
down the road after scrawling a mean graffiti.

The same song, the same song
played the day I lost her. Doors closed
a dusty room the night had flickered
open. Having much in common

as daughters go, we learned new alleys.
She took my side. Walls constructed
of lettered red would watch us cry
in the moonlight, if given the chance, if given
a reason, which, my friends, they were not.

BLANKET PRAISE

I will shut my eyes like a sad man.
I will sign my name in Cyrillic.

They were giving out roses
at the store today. I picked my flower
and went. And all
the children wanted

to know me, and every
Amanda thought me insane,
and sure as the sun
shot out from the East,

the sycophants got with it.
Invisible they were and reluctant
to swallow. Snow at the hemline
soft and bright, another spindled season.

You do not have to talk about it.
Okay. I mean, thank you.

AFTER CAMUS COMES OUT OF A COMA

That's adorable. You're adorable. In the end, we're all going to die, you know, and nothing will be adorable. Sometimes I believe in heaven so that everyone can be adorable. The man who shits on the subway steps? He gets to be adorable. That bitch who mocks how loud you laugh? She gets to be adorable. The pit bull, the vulture, the substandard tip: they too will be adorable. Even I will be adorable. We all will be adorable. Sometimes I believe if we all just believed, we'd all get to be adorable.

LAST NIGHT ALIVE

It was criminal
in its cleverness. Women lost
their memories and grew sullen
before their times.

Beats me,
said the envoy. It's your
telegram: deal with it.

I did and started wearing
fruity antiperspirant, wrestled while tipsy
with a St. Bernard. Silly early on
for Hawaiian-flowered logic, I anchored all
investments to the neighbor's water heater.
That almond hour he calmed my tongue
with wintergreen ovation. We rolled
the windows lower and lower, cruised
like there was slow tomorrow.

Ultra-smoothing aftermath of never
before, decadent prolonging of
tell me again...

We won't get out of this, I warned.
Far off a martyr snickered.
I'm gonna wish that man
right outta' my hair. Put some clothes on
girlie. Nice ones.

ILONA'S EYELIDS

A fondness for the concept of holy water.
Doll stroller, escalator noon. To dip
the tip of a finger in slowness,

cotton shift unwrinkled, to wash
the sleep from a worried face, to bargain
down, to pay.

Infrequently are rumors meant
to ruin one's complexion. Flicker on,
distorted tune. Fabricate,

unravel. The comely altar girl
waits, trips at the door of grace.
Wide-open country. Newfound shipyard.

To rest here without reservations
takes a mean martini. To slip
into light, to dress

one's salad well, a close encounter.
A fake boat, bereft of sound.
The cold, soft lips of belief.

REAL BUTTER

At best, life is hard.
At worst, life is easy.
I believe it is true.
I would like to believe
I believe it is true.
And what about the words
that cannot teach us anything?
I have two new shoes
and neither is practical,
though I love them both,
though I treat them best.
The secret is not hiding
from the music at a party.
We are more important than the secret,
we are more practical than the secret,
we are more secret than the secret,
which makes us the secret.
Which makes us the secret
beauty that at worst is still
a sort of belief. A cheap love
for easy truths is hardly
going to kill you.

CAUTION

In Japanese, my name means love-bell,
tender clang, soft alarm, a heart

murmuring deep in the night
its intimate metal insults.

That I am rapturous
about Disneyland, anything old

with a well-lit gate, I admit
to anyone listening. I admit

a lot of things misunderstood
as wise or colorfully tragic.

"Call me sugar, cause I'm bad for you baby.
Call me tomorrow and I'll ice your ears."

Chocolate almonds, perfect snow,
electrical embezzlement.

Heaven ringing between the cables
the coldest sweet talk we have ever heard.

DEEP SPACE DIALECTIC

My friend's Sigourney Weaver's Assistant and she hasn't seen *Alien*. Not the first, not the second, not the fifth. She has seen no Aliens. "Have you ever seen *Alien*?" I ask her, on a Sunday. She has not nor has she solid plans for this movie to be seen. Sigourney is her "boss." I want Sigourney to be my boss. She has not seen the underwear scene. She'll never see the underwear scene. I start to judge my friend who has a great last name and a killer figure to match. Has she seen *Working Girl*? Will she ever see *Working Girl*? I am no Melanie Griffith, though I like bright things; the film's true hero is Sigourney the Boss. She's a Real Bitch. She has shoulder pads. She hates Melanie Griffith who is blonde and nice. Sigourney didn't get to play nice. She was too busy killing aliens. Aliens in her underwear. Does my friend even wear underwear? Is it white, like Sigourney's? I want to tell her something about power. I want to tell you all about power. Do you want to know what it means to work? Can your shoulders save the planet? I have weaved, I have pleased, I have learned to type on a Brother electronic typewriter. Sometimes my students think I'm a Millennial. I pretend to take this as a compliment. But the fact is, I take nothing for granted. I take everything I can from the burning ship and prepare for the voyage home.

ODE TO CLINT EASTWOOD

This is the land I love.

When I love it is like I am dying
to make a very moving story.

When I move it is like I am dying
to make a story that you love.

Skyline, stranger, bullet hole of light,
they say there is nothing
but unjust clouds to break us

into morning. Not the past,
a promise, a polygraph tricked.
Not bad ibuprofen, not Namaste.

We escape to perfect, empty streets,
angry women. We never escape.

Clint, your very name
sounds like scowling at the sunset.

Do I feel lucky? Only if you do.

2

LIKE GOOD NEWS
FROM A PRETTY GIRL

It was, my friend, a good story. Very, very, very romantic. Several people died. It was black and white, and then it was color. A man got sad, and then he got angry. We all got laid, agreed it was fun. What you thought the story was really about, it wasn't. It was insuperable. A dangerous kid in a rainbow coat kept skating past the market. It freaked us out, always did. Matthew was making a card for his Mom. At this point in time we played "Runaway Bunny" on repeat everyday. Blue sky, brave ears, little thing of whiteness. Where will you lead the patient reader when all of your words are gone? To Holland? Hollywood? Over the plains? When Laura Ingalls was still quite young, her family crossed the prairie. Pa shot a bear and they all ate it. In fact, it was her favorite meal. When I was small I avoided teddies. Animals can't talk so why play with them. People do, so dolls make sense. Evelyn says there's a sweet seam to sadness, that I should try and let it be my guide. What I want to say is, I would love to do that! I would love another story that good people loved. So I find that seam and I choose to pull it. My favorite dress starts to fall apart. I can never go anywhere ever again, spend weekends sewing on buttons. And all the while, I keep telling my friend, I am sorry, but I refuse. I refuse to make this beautiful.

THE HIT

What happened when it rained? A weirdness
all of the town slowed down to know. Parody, a blonde
ambition sopping wet and matted, paralyzed

for seconds, idolized for good. For once, she knew
how a windshield felt. A solitary cinema.
She was a complete sentence written laxly

on the grass. Her shoes, her headscarf.
Her earrings stayed on. I have no interest
in lying here, she told the car

on the side of the road. She'd been so close
to a huge comeback. Words ran down
the gutter all day. When it rained,

a lot of water washed around her
like a story. Imagine
that second so soft you could save it,

a soldier's giddy retreat from routine.
The storm slept on her unframed face
like a fog upon the retina.

Her next big break
would sweep the screen,
a street, a stranger, scripted.

SUNDAY

My hair grew very short and nobody recognized me. My wife walked out of the forest and could not recall my name. Let's call her Marina, cut to commercial, let everyone relax in the limbs for a spell. This means winter has ended at last. A thousand little answers in line for a smile. What decadence cracks with the back of its teeth cannot be made to hearten you. But the fact is, it was a beautiful time. Petals shed from my brand new shirt left patterns all around us.

TAKE HER DOWN

I just want to give you
a run for your money. Slipshod green
on a sleeveless route. Forgetfulness

is a serious term that demands the swiftest
shorthand. A bicycle for the brakeless. A sprinting
rudeness for roads unruled. I do not know

what I am doing, see. I am learning
English for the very last time. Meters grabbed by a sad
stenographer, the actress twice I forgot

to pay, my case is illegible, long past due.
My wry dictation has yet to reach
a finish line worth crossing. Doubly wrong to assume

the worst, I should best keep quiet
shut under the desk. It's levity, not levitation,
that lifts her word for skirt from the page. Traveled

forests, foreign shoes, I just want to tell you
the truth, for once.

EXPLICIT

The nice thing was, we were in love. With enough sparkling water to last the weekend. Songs once filled with shadow shared the sound of vagrant summer, the one where my legs looked better than ever and Gwen Stefani lauded my shades. That really happened. And so must we. And so must Eva Longoria ads at the bus stops of Barcelona. And so must God and the absence of God and Sagrada Família never complete. I am sorry I say "Fuck you!" sometimes when I mean it as a compliment. It is true that my feet are never ever clean. My Buddhist friend named Rachel says I'd make the greatest get-away driver. I buy a Mini Cooper from an artist from Korea. I drive it fast while singing slow. Take the "O" out of poet and you have a little pet. Tack a "B" onto "itch" and your skin calms down. When I stray, eat the "R" with your finest silver. When I slide, sip the "L" in a crystal flute, and then try to discern which one to land on.

CATASTROPHE WAS QUITE POLITE

The way Japan understands
that cute can be strong, cogent,
and misleading, I want to love as though
I slurp from your bowl of anodyne and goat milk.

May the best cloud save us. May the months
of no daylight map all things. To have taken advantage of
cinnamon beaches, rainy nights in a warm sedan,
to have known that there are better places to leave

your heart, or shoes, or both, "We sojourned here,
and as heroes, wept for days that did not warrant
grieving." The world was more real than anyone
could ever call reasonably possible.

But symmetry gets easy. The wind okays
our common friends and takes them out to dinner.
Skies clear the new dessert that no one gets to try.
So that they might soar from the throat of logic,

ice cream headaches, and the color mauve,
birds are allowed to feather trees with luck and paper
money. A girl with a reddish pirouette is about to stain
your sleeve. And if you are just a warm surface

in the end, she will love you, all the same, as a star
shoots itself in the glowing foot, as do we at the threshold
of box-store bliss, minds intent on ruin, lilacs, and the way
to make sure these are never affordable.

ALL EPICS ARE DISAPPOINTING
AND ALL DISAPPOINTMENTS ARE EPIC

Sometimes I like to have feelings just because they are so
impractical. They are electric-green Mary Janes on a hike
and they are my favorite color. Sometimes they make my
calves sad, but my heart is tauter for it. I know a room of
Russian balloons with only room for you. These balloons
are tough—they're Russian—but they're still balloons in
the end. You pick the best and feel its pull; your hand will
not be orphaned. Everything extravagant is pulsing down
your veins. Why scale the night with satin cord? Why
sprint the sequin cliff? In the end, your horse will fall, your
quest will fail to carry. The stars once found so helpful will
start to feel so cold. And yet the yawning sea of sheen
envelops all ambition. Shiver not, ye scrappy child.
Nothing solid saves.

WHITNEY HOUSTON PRONOUNCED DEAD AT 48

Cloud as profile, profile as cloud, so
lovely that even the 1980s glow
like a girl on detox.

Song as skeletal
bathtub treasure, a boy I know, I dream of.
What is it then to be on fire, to rocket

lucky forward? You were sexless
(almost), but when you weren't,
the whole sky sighed soprano.

Body as bureaucracy, body as scandal,
stay in our arms if you dare.
Your sweat, your smile, you're always always

never, all at once.

NOBODY'S WINTER

It was nobody's winter, the shoes, the shoes
that brought us here were earned today.

My mouth mispronounced meat.
Spoonful of sea salt and a pillaged lime.
There were grape leaves we couldn't
get to, an attic without a home, and all the time

I kept saying, "Whatever they tell you, don't forget."
You forgot. The ocean swallowed. And my tongue
pretended to care. Or maybe it was the stupid
ruse of my own impossible quiet. Hey, kiddo,

hey, God, did you think this was going to happen?
The ladies selling lotion found us really, really funny.
Everything obvious smelled of ore
and fingerprints from Toronto. If you want to know

the truth, know the numbers that I come from,
know empiricism, speed, flowers buried in
the dark. I was never afraid of the silent,
see. I had sacrificed the handsomest months

of my life. The shore cleared out so slowly
I couldn't believe that you went with it.
Like a blind child who takes the arm of his brother,
who is also blind.

LIFE AFTER RUGBY

I.

As the grizzly charm of circumstance had worn itself
slender, and the carriers at the post office modeled
woolen pants, her options were few. Die or do not.
The sound of boots through snow in the dark

surrounded all the city. She had red hair,
nice legs, a silly way of sneezing. You'd know it
if she snuck inside your hole. She'd like it
if the whole place surged with light—

suddenly the subtleties of algebra get frisky.
The common factors each stand up and nip you
on the neck. And angles, bitter angles?
You'd find they really dig you.

Not a doorway bent on keeping you out,
but a cheekbone shyly brushing your wrist. One day
the sky turned carbonated, went to the head too quickly.
Money was lost, then found, then trashed,

and flatscreens flew from the roofs. Her ankle bracelet
snapped. She spilled into a puddle. Her coins
escaped into moonlit air and owls assessed the mess.
The whole world was watching, the whole world was

winning. To have won and lost, to have watched
and learned the ropes up which daredevils climb,
of which neighbor girls go skipping ahead as though
their lives depended on it, to then waste one's day,

one's valid ticket, on the leanest bite of woe? "Whatev,"
she said, and cocked her head, exonerating no one.
With the best of her Sugar Ray Leonard bob,
she weaved beyond the traffic.

Symphony, prosperity, the loose mares of time.
Homily of hominy, of long dreams and lime.
Outside her glowing loungecar, igloos in space.
And trapped below her collar? A gift of dark lace.

II.

Heart of slumbering, liquid trees. Bitten
apple falling. There are millions of suns.

It is morning, cold. The neighbors stare
at the neighbors.

I am happy because it is the only way
to beat you, friend. I am happy also because

I am a happy little girl.

When a sawed-off shotgun is properly used
on a softly dirty Monday,

where a mother and father intend to learn
the numbers of a room,

how can anyone hazard a guess—
a groom—a full-grown body

breaking? There are things
one shouldn't covet, love.

These are men worth semi-crouching for.
Some go alone, while others share

their invisible rooms with others.
Do you hate the way the happy hate?

Can you tell me the street
where you were born?

III.

some

slaughter, sweetie, some no-regrets
some sad and bootless thing in the night
some anecdote about hidden bread
some cases here cannot be cured

IV.

black lake of good below
the soft of our hands so smart and blind

when we learned to read the harvest
little did we know

of arias, and attics, of a man's
gentle climb

down yet another woman
in yet another town

to yet another sonnet
in yet another gown

and the sweetness she called
from the back of the room

from the back of her throat
from the cool of her tomb

cannot will itself to work that way
today, tonight, or any day

and tho she be wise
and full of grace

hot ribbon cinched
about her waist

thick accent trained
like Cotillard

in silver hose and leotard
turned satin robe and liquid trunks

weightless boots and leather gloves
a cavalcade outside the ring

the will to knock down anything
hit or miss or kiss or spit

lips and legs and pools to split
is a city in Croatia where she had been

the girls were untraveled
the roads very thin

V.

You'd know it if she snuck inside your hole. She'd like it
if the whole place surged with light. More how than when,
more Venn than Zen, this version was true. Fall or fly off.
The sound of birds through snow in the dark

surrounded all the city. They had strong wings,
clean beaks, a bitter way of singing. They'd know it
if you snuck inside her hole. You'd like it
if the whole place surged with light.

VI.

Sometimes I want to rip you in half
to prove that I am hungry.

Waffles! Sharks! Motorcycles!
A lot of good ways to go.

Some went alone, and some shared their invisible
rooms with others.

This deliberate tree I grow for you
every time you take my hand.

VII.

History, hilarity, the strewn blooms of rhyme.
Holiday of holy days, of cold lens and crime.

To have won and lost, to have watched and learned,
to have hidden the handsomest months of a life,
to have lived for months on stolen snow,
to have followed the rules of an empty room.

One day the sky turned carbonated, went to the head
too quickly. Money was lost, then found, then trashed,
and flatscreens flew from the roofs. The whole world
was watching, the whole world was watching.

Shutter
Shutter
Shutter
Shutter

Let me be your heavyweight.

3

EUPHORIA TAKES ONE FOR THE TEAM

A brave dog will teach you to swim
and Jim will fix your furnace.

Song will wake the spiders
you have hidden in your sleep.

Your arms, lovers, long at the wrist
will wrestle with a hubcap.

Change dropped from another's suit
will glisten if you keep it.

I LIKE THAT YOU DON'T CARE ABOUT MONEY

I am someone who's good with money. I know where it is and where it's not. I know how to save it, how to spend it, how to earn it all back the day it's gone. I don't like that I am good with money because I do not like the money itself. I am good with money the same way I am good with workaholics, the way I'm good with supersad people who often want to die, the way I'm good with sore losers and good with oral surgery and good with lo-calorie kettle corn. I am not sure you are good with money. You sleep like it does not exist. It's the same as if I believed in God, believed He watched my every move, but you were one of those merry atheists who don't know anyone's watching. I'm watching you. I want to learn, to be good with someone very good. I would give you all my money if you gently asked me for it, but I'd also surely make a lot more of it once you're gone. Once one knows what to learn, being good with gone is worthless. Once one knows what is gone, being good can cost a lot.

THROUGH MY TEETH

I was lying all alone and the cars didn't know me.
The old man I am always thinking
should cry for once, for all, upon death,
came back to chew the coast away
with his brand new set of discount solutions.

And the motiveless levity of little girls
didn't piss me off. Not this time. I was the back page
bride of a worn-out life, a flatbed truck
with the town at its britches.

Though I ached in the knees, I'd patch it up, learn
to do remarkable things, remember the names
of childhood rivals: Washington, Moss, Amanda Seece.
The thing is, it was devastating to be saved
so very quickly. I was writing home

in my travel veil; the freeway lit up
satin soft. Like New York, but with hollandaise—
that was how it tasted. I could've died there,
believe me. I can tell the difference.

NOT FOR PROFIT

To see the sun unmatte the room without her was upsetting. A golden outline squared the bed, the gin in the freezer hedged its bets. There used to be more to eat in here than the house of your sugar-free sisters. You were not wrong, and were not startled, to find this corner of earth so sweet. A crusty schoolbook explained the angles. Handsome letters hid under the desk. Joy dense as a welcome snowfall, she framed your name in official pink. Our bliss is prettier in writing off the lucent face of God, she said. But after absence, aspartame. Because after all, she has left this chapel.

"LITTLE BOY"

Shut your eyes, sailor, let the long ago
swim. An ache unnamed,
an August storm, torn from the book

about birds in flight, you were looking
good, a real good looker,
riddled with blue, inescapable light.

There's a first time for everything,
kiddo. And when all of it falls
at your earth-burnt feet, remember:

the end is the easy part.
Dropped from the palms
of a depthless sky, you were thinking

no one would notice you. Blind
we'd become as though helpless
to beauty. Blind we remain

to the soles of our sleep.
Having always had the time
to stop the upset, set the table, paint

a pattern of escape in the ash-glittered air,
your pants come undone between
deathcloud and promise. Down deep

where we know there is nothing
to silence, a seed that year
cannot quietly drown

will push past playground dirt to find
a sacred place of water.
And you, you with the bright excuse,

buttoned shirt and zippered past,
fall and rise a thousand miles
beyond what was and could be yours.

BLESSED ARE THEY, THE CINEMATIC

When I was young, I was Catholic, watched few non-cartoons. One was a live action feature film on the life of the young St. Francis. Francis returning from the Crusades and his mother softly crying, Francis tossing his noble clothes from a tower over town, Francis taming a tiny bird, Francis with no shoes on. Francis sings in a gentle tenor, fleeing his jerk of a dad. He comes across Clare about one third through, and that's where it gets good. Clare is the perfect Seventies Saint—long Breck hair and braless. "They call me...Clare!" Clare declares when smiling Francis asks. Her hair is blonde, her eyes are blue, she's brutal as she turns her head. So brutal and pretty that no one can have her—not even Francis (not like he tries). As a nun, she follows him into the hills, a white and silent shadow. As a nun, her waist-long hair is gone, which made me want the movie to end. In the end, everyone's singing outside and the clouds divide like lovers. There are few lessons I recall more clearly than the lessons I learned from this feature film.

FAITH EQUIVALENT TO AIRPLANE

I'll make it up for you: two wings
on the way to happiness or some other
distant color, the ghost that goes the same way
we do, ghost-blue and lofty-headed, a little bit
lost and dangerous. This is faith, like a pheromone,
floating through the attics, the top floor of a ruined
heart, filled with bits and pieces, a peaceful
project for engineers, a ghetto-fab apartment.
These are the final minutes before we land
the deal of a lifetime. What else would you like
me to tell you, world? I'll make up a plan you can't
refuse, a trashy jaunt through the wilderness.
In this happy time for headphones, plane of tame
entendres, I plan to make you mine within
the limits of a logo. This cabin-frozen love
for cockpit, for always, for pilot-lit deliverance
basement deep, these wings
will not collapse overnight, not now, right
in the spring of things. This skin, chilled
to the musk of touch, will ribbon,
will cloud the alkaline sky.

LOVE POEM FROM DETROIT

to know that the grass sweats more than we do
that people wear perfume that smells like grass

the long dream of a true downtown
will wrestle us together

in the darkness in the music in the moon and in
the walls

in the music is the knowledge is the
legible persuasion

is the only way to Canada to follow
cryptic laws

where will you go and what will you do
and who will you be without me

your own imperious unicorn
and no one around to show

LIVING PROOF

I could have set you free. If almonds hadn't
made me skinny, the world would look a lot
wholesomer. Hold on to my bag of ruffled
streetmaps. Here, a passage. Waterfall
waffles. There, a pile of homeless bottles.
A world less easy

would finish me. I would deserve this,
to know great weight, to kneel, to fall
from the skirt of the city.

ODE TO MIKE TYSON

Sometimes I wanna say no
just so I can say it like you do.
As though nothing can be affirmed,
as though you can't run into the ocean.

No. The appeased aren't onto us.
No. A small, triumphant church.
No. A dog chasing a glove
on a street I can't remember.

Freedom is only lonely
when you let it be.
The heat precedes the fire.
A boy precedes the heat.

Sometimes a lake is really a sea,
your prize pigeon beheaded.
Unmask my pet illusions.
Devastate the world.

NEVER LANDING

You shall have a shadow. You shall dress in gold.
When Peter thought his friend would die,
he was more than a little impatient. Belief

was a slippery, worn out thing, the sky
a course of improvement at best.
So what next? Nothing's the matter
here. You know how to cloud,

how to color the plot-lines. Heaven
is like a calm hotel where cherries
paper the sitting rooms. And flight?

Not just allegory, not just all a great
reason for secrets. You kept
giving away the good silver. You kept
quiet for long enough. Medicine

to drink atop a mountain of nirvanas,
poison that one takes to circumvent
the next applause, suddenly,

you will want to tinker with the details.
As that hot tease, Tiger Lily, finger-licks
the entrance of a thought, in a lobby,
that is just now being born.

WHOOPI WILL ALWAYS BE CENTER SQUARE

Right now I am on a plane and there is nothing mundane about it. Cumulus looms, surrounding sky. Surround sound in a dimming place. Laughter, Twizzlers, moving light. What was then was then, is very important, but not so much that we can't have now. Gertrude Stein loved tiny words, she caressed the nouns till they came in waves. Outside my plane is a Care Bear house, and nobody cares but me. Rainbows have never bloomed from my abs, but at times I have felt that way. One night I heard your manly voice and imagined your boyish sleeping. That night I slept so happy I felt as though I could vomit stars. Have you ever felt that way? Do you love the life you waken? My best friend Jake knows a lot about culture, at least the kind that counts. Sometimes we talk about Hollywood Squares and ardently swap our childhoods, how you stare at the blacktop flat on your stomach stunned at how it smells. You wonder, how badly have I been hurt? Will somebody come to check? What I'm trying to say is, being this high doesn't hurt my ears anymore. I have heard the call of ambivalent birds and still fall fast asleep. I have stared at a word like "laughter" until I know it's spelled correctly. I have left the curtains open, always, and I've faced the face of the kindest man.

HONEYMOON THAT NEVER HAPPENED

Let's say red.
Let's say trickling southward Sunday briefs.
Let's be brief, fiercely genius.

Let's take the diamond out of the box.

Plainly, we would wed the world
entire were it original. Ready to serve,
the season thickens. Ready
or not, the winter shrinks.

Why else does faith belittle
those who spread their sheets
so thinly? The rings rush down
a thousand rooms, a finger's
worth of brilliance.

The trick is how to trick
yourself. The heart *is* rock
until it is thrown.

IMPERVIOUS TO AVALANCHE

Waiting for light to shake
only always

would we smile. I wish
to sleep

in perfect snow, die of sweet
collision, halfway to a heavy sky

and infinitely held. You say
you think I'd live through this,

you love as though it's proven.
An excavated craving

for precision keeps me warm.
We curve as though

contrived of light, climb
as though it cures us.

Only and always hidden
blind, with sturdy shovel lifted.

GENTLY NOW, THE REVOLUTIONS

I was going to tell you where to go.
And the trees that lined
the sidewalks would be waiting there
like friends. One of them has hot cocoa
and a scrappy little hat and you promise
not to lose the map of festivals
he's made you. How on earth, as it is
elsewhere, will you find the next engagement?
A crepe paper arrow strikes us all
as a waste. Far from the silent corridors
where nurses meet with teachers, where leaves
are all the likeness of a fallen letter 'k,'
if all else fails, plan to meet in Kansas,
Krakow, Kyoto, Kokomo Beach. Enter the house
with calm persistence, sure that no one
real survives. There are many truths
with which to wager war on the world
unjustly. The jaded dream you dare
deem joyful smudges doorknobs, closet
shelves. Climbing down a rotted branch, down
a quickly branching year, the friend
you've made of yourself, the only
answered prayer that proves unknowable,
is hurt, has been often hurt, and has great reason
to be lost. I was going to tell you
where to go to find some fresh azaleas.
This time around, the earth
has saved a space for a place to live.

4

DRIVE

The birth of an engine soft in your ears embellishing its provenance, a starless past that proves irredeemably forgone; orange moon, safe hands, a sudden pedal swooning; a shift into someplace dark, sincere, a solid daring duty. When else does the soul go slack, slick its bangs straight back to see? What right have we right now to say that time takes sides to taunt us? To hear the stir of a Suburu and call it to the night, to steer the heart with a hardened palm and quantify its relevance, to stake one's claim on an unpaved place and pray that it is worth it— isn't this what the wonderful women who didn't raise us were always raving about? This leather and heat and soft seat wishing this rain and a midday singing so long this more than 3,000 miles more than Alaska more than my mother this drivetrain talent for transaxle searching this engine turning and turning again this torque approach to front-wheel living I was never your slushbox beautiful nothing I was agency movement clutch clutch clutch I was 500 hp gold and you know it the place it was I came from on that deathless night I came.

SIMPLE PLANS

Deeply concerned about water, starlight,
the home where we should have been
all along, but were not; waiting for fountain soda
to fill our manly full-liter mornings, manifestoes

minnowing forward, every America
making its mark; the last thing on our minds
was the memory of bonnets, thought bubbles floating
past unsold meats. Bright and vital, bright and vicious,

a California crime scene caught on film,
every penumbra was priced to move
according to its predators. Planets traced the patterned lot
and we reread the signs. That space-heated season

we knew would not return despite our chivalries,
the inclement hour our blankets burned
like comets before our eyes, we awoke to tissue paper,
petals of feeling. Our tired hands

unwrapped like gifts. What had been lost
beyond the sky, a galaxy of excess, a mountain climbed
that crumbled in the palms beyond the shore—
we wondered why the atmosphere adorned itself in data.

The streets, like ticker-tape, ribboned with reasons,
the race of our hearts as we fell again.
Out of line with logic, into fashioned
sprays of distant grief, ambrosial poise,

the pennies and the plumage that stole into the city
left our heads unmade with fear. We thought it was over
when the clowns showed up. Crowds without a crisis
raffled off a used prescription. A sound from the station

blue enough to refill the world anew.
"History is finishing," we yawned
by the glowing snack table. A close call, a lucky night,
a lovely mackintosh slick with dirt; music

from the lobby, unbelievable bread and ballroom fire.
We dipped into bowls of beige and then returned our hands
to our faces. Recreation, plenitude, irresistible
reasons to spill. Irresistible reasons to pull together

what was missing. With the rhythmic grass
of hula girls, we shimmied down the runway.
Deeply concerned, we launched into space
our fat, loud, carnivorous vowels.

THE LONELY ART
OF COLLECTING OLIVES

Watch to be sated. The brain nests
a splintered thought that seeds
its own creation. A hand white

with secret buds extends a leathered
leaf. With the sun on your eyelids, clutch
what is dripping, dropping

forward in flesh-colored waves.
A new ground is sweetly broken.
Shield your face from the sonorous

heat. Enough will be your lot
to inherit. Less will be the branch
at your feet.

THE SPRING OF THINGS

The man—the salesman—at the mattress store was beautiful. And very loved. But he loved only mattresses, their beautiful contusions, their floral sighs as bodies broke them in on winter nights. Or maybe he loved them for how they made him fall in love with people—the joker gone quiet as he closed his eyes, the waitress who vowed she'd "never get off." His lover, however, never quite got it. She bragged whenever she got the chance of how she could sleep "anywhere." She dared the man to nap upon her newly-vacuumed carpet. "Here's your chance," she mouthed across the candle-scented air. There were flowers at his door and a hornet on his sleeve, and still the song of coiled springs was all that he could process. Passion begins with dread, he said, to whomever would stop and listen. The coward hour his lover left, his bedroom started sinking. Every door in the house awoke and swam itself ajar. And the man, our friend, who was once so loved, and his new, capacious mattress? He has dried his face, put on his clothes, replaced the damaged flatsheet. He has left his bed for the grace of the sale, the simple sound of staying awake, aware of the beautiful denseness beneath.

ODE TO TAXI DRIVER

I want an RC cola and a quiet man.
I don't want to talk, not tonight.

And all the immiscible cash in the street
couldn't make me talk to you.

And all the immutable red from my sleeve
couldn't shake the neighbors.

I got mean veins, but a kind heart.
The kind keeping trying to talk to me.

The kind of hair you could braid
into a noose is spilling down your pillow.

What I spread is not paternalism,
is not your father's father's pride.

I am not your father, but I am cinematic.
Not everything is easy.

The flowers I bought are ash in the sink
and do not look like flowers.

You talkin' to me? I didn't think so.
And the angels grind their last dulcet notes.

MELODY, SPEED,
AND A MAN WORTH MANNING

I have known them as flashing thunder-stealers, echo-fed
and friendly. I have called to mind some thirty-plus
purples and dare to pin one close to your ear. My lanky

statistician, so stern, so storm-ready, a thousand
lighted houses rush across the night to greet you. Little-
known apothecaries lure you to the door. I would stumble

if so doing meant the sky would smell of oranges
or that somewhere someone watching would see fit
to paint a portrait. But listen to how dulcetly I play

the game of catch up. Time is on my side and finds
direction in my frill. Roulade of lucent rationalizations,
ocean sad with conjugated rooms, the schooner is

shifting; the race is not rigged. The season of fallen birds
that I was too in love to notice comes as close to home
as the wind allows. Count yourself among

the counted. Say you know me, and say it again.

CANOE

Maybe you didn't know this about me, but I have a canoe. I can't operate it alone, but I do have paddles. If you have my number and want to go, just call me in the next couple days. We can share some sunscreen and I'll tell you stories. How last week I went out on a dinner date with a man from Montreal. He was in town to check on planes—to "proof the planes," he told me. He was an aeronautic engineer and he paid for our sangrias. His father had died, I learned that night, found Jesus toward the end. "God is like crutches," the Quebecois said. "Does that mean you don't believe?" I admired the scar above his eyebrow. Later we split a fancy shake. It was his idea. I didn't sleep with him. The night was so hot that we never held hands.

ODE TO ROMAN HOLIDAY

I too fell and the fall was filled. Light,
creamy ache from the ceiling, followed us
to the library. Musk pillowed the stairway walls

and quiet soon caught fire. Here you put
your arms and legs as time escapes the cranny.
These are pajamas. They're for sleeping over in, you see.
Under clouds, outdoor mobiles. Gazebo dreams of

caregiving dogs. Wendy and John learn how to fly;
it's easy. It's an experiment. Later on, the ones they love
to listen to grow worried. Loud, slender, something else,

a jar within a story, a tinking thing, a thinking sting, a star
that follows after. The princess wakes and recites a lesson.
Growing up means calming down. Borders crossed
below her head from lands of sound unequaled.

But oh, the smell of waffle cones, the restless newsman's
hovering past. There, she almost swallowed it all. Now,
she says, it is *soo* over.

INVISIBLE MEN

Lately I've stopped seeing rich white men. When they come my way, I only see what happens to hide behind them—the velvet folds of a lobby curtain, a happy homeless dog, the abstract art on an abstract wall that no one bothered to sign. Such blindness (or vision) is an enviable asset, though I suppose there are those who take affront. I can't know for sure, but had I the chance, I would stand on my toes behind them. I would cup my palm and whisper warmly: *Please, don't take it personally. I just happen to see right through you.*

THE WORLD

The world does not take place in the shower.
Though maybe her world does. The world is full
of snacks and smut, unheated basements, pain.
The world is full of places where there is no basement
or where basements are the world that you know
and love. The known world is notably not the world
in love, or loved while confessing state lines.
Let's all agree that the state wields power.
Let's all ignore from our sage mint showers. As a child,
I was scared of our grandma's basement. Bad things
had and would have happened. A world replete
with bad things happening, repeating
themselves like a cotton rose. Our loved world
would love to be happy, would be happy to love
the smut, the sage. Then a man dies quiet and another
dies loud, a boy lies dead for more than four hours.
The world is not afraid to watch, is full
of carpeted reasons to wait. The world underground
is thorny, smells, and is much more loved
than the world we know. The world has wasted
a lot of water. Power is wasting the city sun.
Let's all confess full on for the world, for ourselves
still wet with unknowable heat, that the world we
shower with lies, with snacks, is the whitest
world one can painfully know. Let us rise
as much in rhyme as at risk. Let us scare ourselves
with this world on loan, our world we eat
and love and shame.

CLOSURE

While moving out of the yellow house, I found your soul in the basement. It was dusty, in a suitcase, but perfectly functional. My dog looked over. I showed it to him. He sniffed it out then hid in the laundry. I thought about whether I'd use it or not. My own was old but in pretty good shape. In the right kind of light, it could even look beautiful. Could a brand new room have the right kind of light? Can a brand-clean blue bring the best type of clouds? Dream on, little duck, little billfold of ache. Wax on, and then off, about patterns of breaking. You know how to scar, how to star the whole city; you lower your face to the pool that consumes. Wipe out the sun from your eyes, indeed. Rip off that tie you were wearing to please him. And if, in the end, we are not indifferent, smooth out the seams that scheme from below. You wanna get a piece of it? Marry the wary. You wanna go home? God bless you for wanting.

WORLD CUP

Let life eat you.
Say you are thankful
because you are and because
that is what one says right now.

Summer loss at the hem
of your dreams, sink your past
on the kindest ship.

You, too, will slip into sun.
You, too, will be kicked awake.

ODE TO CALIFORNIA CHROME

I started, and I got my start.
Strangers watched, or cried,
made bets, and did not
seem so strange to me.

I was given a bracelet
from a gift shop in Chicago, I won
admission to a hill of trees, went blonde,
bought a house, sang songs to my dog
while sweeping the stairs of his good dog fur.

O, effort, O glory, O old desperation,
O anything sweaty and foaming at the mouth,
defeat is bitterest to those
whom victory sweetly
clouded once, or twice.

I do not believe in God, or anyone
to whom I'd owe my afterlife.
But I say, sweet steed, track to track,
you are no golden ruin. Everyone wanted

to see you fly, and wanting
something that badly only made you
more like everybody else;
as anything worth believing
in, every belief the run made bright

bursts back to a day so dirty
every one of us swallowed our fears
and said, "This is the first thing
we ever expected. This
is the end." And we race on.

FROM THE FIRST BOOK OF FAR AWAY

A mind littered with happy music, a heart broke
into quieted halves—what you take from the platter
is on the house. A shingled sequel, rain-swept sleeves.

Long forearms will lift you up to a place
the paint left clean of prints. Fingers spread
the slogans, over fences, under the dampened loft.

What happens here is memory—yours, to be exact.
A need to read the landmarks, a safe
cracked by fastidious hands. You will not qualify

everything, and you shouldn't, even the night
it storms. Rooms crowd beneath the station as trains
stall for towns at a time. This is your country.

There are no shortcuts. The pages turn and you forget.

I AM, AS ALWAYS,

eventually your ribbon house,
your soggy sugar cone, the wrist you break
with a swollen heart on a walk with another person.

I am all the time consumable, clarified
butter in a bowl of milk. Free like the haircut, sunset,
blowjob, that makes you feel a bit better
about yourself. Girls making out with hitmen
slowly gentrify the city. Women making out
with handbags start to billboard glassy homes.
Maybe you don't notice this. Nowhere dear

do you make demands. Downtown, at nighttime,
a boy spinning fire fills the trees
with ghosts you believe in. A broker
hangs her hat on her head; the crumbling lion
loses an ear. The rain wet coupon
you thought had expired swirls its way
down the playground steps.

There are places where the precipice
of reason is the reason. Hold on
to my wreckage or, please, let me go.

I HAVE NOT BEEN CHARGED
FOR THE CLOSET

that was filled with birds, silt, gloves,
and the dullness of pedals. My heart was clean

from the very first. My hands were ready
and opened like gifts. In sleep, the sound of hours rushed
across the street to ravish me.

I have made light of many things
and that's why we can see in here.

ACKNOWLEDGMENTS

I would like to thank Rebecca Bridge and Niel Rosenthalis for their insights in the final stages of preparing this collection. Thanks also to Gold Wake editors Nick Courtright and Kyle McCord for their faith in my manuscript and fidelity to my vision. Mad gratitude to Amy Wright, Gillian Parrish, and Cynthia Barounis for their thoughtful feedback across the years. Finally, I am indebted to the following journals and literary forums that granted many of my poems a home, though on occasion with variant titles.

ALIVE (Never Landing; The Spring of Things; The Reason the Moon Moves; The Lonely Art of Collecting Olives; Melody, Speed, and a Man Worth Manning)

American Literary Review (Like Good News from a Pretty Girl)

American Poetry Journal (Simple Plans)

American Poetry Review (Ilona's Eyelids)

Boston Review (The World; Euphoria Takes One for the Team; From the First Book of Far Away)

Conduit (Deep Space Dialectic; Gently Now, the Revolutions)

DIAGRAM (Nobody's Winter; After Camus Comes Out of a Coma)

Gold Wake Live (Ode to Taxi Driver; Caution; Last Night Alive)

Handsome (Closure; Blessed Are They, the Cinematic)

Harp & Altar (Blanket Praise; Sunday)

Interim (Through My Teeth; Love Poem from Detroit)

Jerry (Drive; Impervious to Avalanche)

Juked (Ode to Mike Tyson; Follow the Girl in the Red Boots)

Kadar Koli (Ode to California Chrome; Women & Children; Explicit)

Ninth Letter ("Little Boy"; Canoe)

Parthenon West Review (I Am, As Always)

Privacy Policy: Anth. of Surveillance Poetics (I Like That You Don't Care About Money)

Sonora Review (Whoopi Will Always Be Center Square)

The Rumpus (Invisible Men; Real Butter; Honeymoon That Never Happened)

U City Review (Ode to Clint Eastwood; All Epics Are Disappointing...)

Zone 3 (I Have Not Been Charged for the Closet)

ABOUT GOLD WAKE PRESS

Gold Wake Press, an independent publisher, is curated by Nick Courtright and Kyle McCord. All Gold Wake titles are available at amazon.com, barnesandnoble.com, and via order from your local bookstore. Learn more at goldwake.com.

Available Titles:

Erin Stalcup's *Every Living Species*
Glenn Shaheen's *Carnivalia*
Frances Cannon's *The High and Lows of Shapeshift Ma and Big-Little Frank*
Justin Bigos' *Mad River*
Kelly Magee's *The Neighborhood*
Kyle Flak's *I Am Sorry for Everything in the Whole Entire Universe*
David Wojciechowski's *Dreams I Never Told You & Letters I Never Sent*
Keith Montesano's *Housefire Elegies*
Mary Quade's *Local Extinctions*
Adam Crittenden's *Blood Eagle*
Lesley Jenike's *Holy Island*
Mary Buchinger Bodwell's *Aerialist*
Becca J. R. Lachman's *Other Acreage*
Joshua Butts' *New to the Lost Coast*
Tasha Cotter's *Some Churches*
Hannah Stephenson's *In the Kettle, the Shriek*
Nick Courtright's *Let There Be Light*
Kyle McCord's *You Are Indeed an Elk, but This Is Not the Forest You Were Born to Graze*
Kathleen Rooney's *Robinson Alone*
Erin Elizabeth Smith's *The Naming of Strays*

ABOUT THE AUTHOR

Eileen G'Sell received an MA from the University of Rochester and an MFA in creative writing from Washington University in St. Louis. In 2012 she co-cofounded The Hinge, an award-winning art gallery and creative project space. Her cultural criticism, essays, and poetry can be found in *Salon*, *VICE*, *Boston Review*, *DAME*, *DIAGRAM*, *Conduit*, *Ninth Letter*, *Secret Behavior*, and the *Denver Quarterly*, among others; and she was awarded the 2013 American Literary Review prize for poetry. Her chapbooks are available from Dancing Girl and BOAAT Press, and she is a features editor for The Rumpus. She currently teaches rhetoric and poetry at Washington University, and creative writing for the Prison Education Project at Missouri Eastern Correctional Center. She lives in St. Louis and New York.

CPSIA information can be obtained
at www.ICGtesting.com
Printed in the USA
FFOW03n1253200218
45193808-45721FF